A TALE OF TROY

A TALE OF TROY

BY

JOHN MASEFIELD

LONDON
WILLIAM HEINEMANN LTD.
1932

PRINTED IN GREAT BRITAIN
AT THE WINDMILL PRESS

TO
MY WIFE

I Thank the beautiful Speakers:

SYBIL HERIZ-SMITH

ROSE BRUFORD

DULCIE BOWIE

RONALD WATKINS

JUDITH MASEFIELD

AMY REAN

and

ALBERT FOWLER

*who first told this tale
on Midsummer Night,* 1932

THE TAKING OF HELEN

Menelaus, the Spartan King,
Was a fighting man in his early spring,
With a war-cry loud as a steer's bellow,
And long yellow hair, so the poets sing.

But he wearied of war, and longed to bide
In quiet at home by his fireside ;
He wooed and wedded the beautiful Helen
And carried her home to be his bride.

And little delight was hers, poor thing,
To be tied till death to the Spartan King,
She moved in the cage of the Spartan court
Like a bright sea-bird with a broken wing.

Paris came from a Trojan glen,
The prince of the world's young famous men,
With a panther's eye and a peacock air,
Even the goddesses wooed him then.

He came from Troy to the Spartan port,
He moored his galley: he rode to court

In a scarlet mantle spanged with gold
On a delicate stallion stepping short.

Helen and he knew each from each
That a red ripe apple was there in reach,
The loveliest girl and the loveliest lad
Ready to learn and ready to teach.

He said "O Helen, why linger here
With the King your husband year by year?
What life is this to a star like you,
The brightest star in the atmosphere?

O beautiful girl, I love but you,
And a life of love is your rightful due:
Come with me over the sea to Troy,
Where Queens shall ride in your retinue."

She said to him, "O Paris, my own,
Since I married him I have lived so lone
That life is bleak as a withered bone.
O take me hence into light and life,
My spirit within me turns to stone."

Then Paris said, "But we will not fly
Like thieves that have heard a step draw nigh.

2

You are the Queen and I am I;
I'll carry you off to my golden ship
At noonday under your husband's eye."

So it was planned, so it was done,
Paris and she were there at one,
The sentry bribed and the door undone,
With a waiting ship and a rising wind
Helen was off with Priam's son.

THE GOING TO TROY

He took her to Troy, the windy town
Where the exploit gave him great renown.
Helen was bright as a golden crown.
But Menelaus in Sparta swore:—
"This shall topple their towers down."

Agamemnon, his brother, vowed:—
"Troy shall be sacked that is so proud.
The sites of her temples shall be ploughed.
We have waited long, but the cup is brimmed,
The glory of Asia shall be bowed."

By lying and threats and fraud and force
He gathered his ships and spears and horse.
As many as thorns on April gorse
He sent them aboard in Argos Bay,
And away to Troy they took their course.

But difficult fortunes wait on ships,
For the winds may blow their sails to strips
And the waves may knock their planks to chips,
Or the wind may stop their going at all,
And Death come salt on the seamen's lips.

4

It was not triumph and prize they found,
But a wind that kept them harbour-bound
Week after week in Kalkis Sound,
Dying of fever, under a curse,
Till a tenth were under the burial mound.

What did they do, that might avail
To appease the gods that the ships might sail?
A horror that makes the cheek turn pale,
A horror that Agamemnon did:
But the Queen herself shall tell the tale.

KLYTAIMNESTRA

(*Enters*)

I am that Klytaimnestra whom Agamemnon wedded,
Queen of a beautiful land in a city rich in gold.
Would that my happy fortune might strike me suddenly
    dead.

The cause of the Trojan war was not Queen Helen,
That lovely fool of a girl, with her painted boy,
But lust for the spoil of the peaceful Trojan towns,
And the vanity of Agamemnon, the King,
Who raged, after all those years, because King Priam
Was chosen to walk before him at Zeus's rites.
Those children, drunken with youth, were but the pretext.

Such was the "righteous war" that my husband preached
    of.
And all the youth of all the cities and kingdoms
Went at the bidding of Agamemnon to Troy.

We women and little children and aged men
Were left behind to the work that the fighters left,
To raise the food and wine that the fighters wasted
And forge the weapons to kill some woman's dear one.

6

Months passed by, with never a message, but orders
To press more youths, to hurry them on to the war.
And the youths marched singing away and none returned.

Never a message of love came, none, but rumours
From each blind beggar that passed, of ruin and death.
And the daily bread of our lives was pain of mind.

Then, after months, a herald came from my husband,
Giving his ring as sign, speaking these very words:—
"The spearmen and all the ships are drawn in a port
    ashore,
Waiting to fall on Troy when the Trojans least expect us.
But, while we wait for the day,
Fortune provides a means of linking our House of Atreus
With the House of Peleus' self, that the Halves of Greece
    be linked.
We plan that our Daughter Iphigenia be married
To Achilles, Prince of Phthia, thus linking the kingdoms.
Therefore, Queen, we will, that you send our Daughter to
    Aulis
Under the guard we send, that so she may marry the
    prince."

I sent my darling Daughter away to Aulis.

It was all a lie of the King's, from end to end;
There was no marriage prepared; the fleet was wind-
    bound,
Unable to sail for Troy, and the food was scarce,
The camp was sickly, mutinous; quarrels were hot.
My Husband knew, when he sent that message of lies,
That within two weeks his League would dissolve in rage.
So he schemed to kill my girl as a sacrifice,
That the gods might change the wind and the fleet set sail.

My Daughter went with the guards, thinking she went to
    be bride.
They say that her Father smiled, that his plot had thriven
    so well.
She was decked as they deck cows, she was bound as they
    bind beasts,
And he and his filthy priests prayed loud to the gods to
    hear;
And a thousand men stood near; not one of them lifted
    hand;
In the light, on the sea-sand, he killed his child with a
    prayer.
And after he burned her there, and took an oath at her
    dust
That all should be faith and trust, since brotherly love was
    best.

And the wind swung round to the west; they shouted
    there in their joy.
They left a poor little tomb behind on the trampled
    beach.
With singing and merry speech those heroes sailed to-
    wards Troy.

If there be any Curse, Fury or Evil
Able to leap from the Hurt Heart, to follow
The causer of the Hurt, and grapple, biting
Until the Fangs have riven his very life,
Let such curse follow Agamemnon always
And all his men.
              Open, you kennels of Hell,
Come all you hounds of hell, red-eared, red-eyed,
Come Quarrel, Insult, Outrage, Misery, Shame,
Come lolling-tongued, tireless, hellish-hearted,
Hunt them down shrieking to untimely Death.

This hatred is but misery, daylong, nightlong.
Vengeance will not bring back my little daughter.
Would that a happy fortune would strike me dead!

THE SPEARMAN

You have heard the lady, making her complaints.
I was at Aulis: the gods were angry with us:
They had to be appeased by the King's child.
When that was done, at once the whole curse lifted,
The gods were with us, we sailed, we were successful.

We sacked the little cities in league with Troy.
Then we landed in force three miles from Troy,
Drew up our ships and fenced them with ditch and wall.
We learned, later, that Hektor, Priam's son,
Urged that all Troy should fall on us with fire
Then, while we dug; but old fools in the council
Caused Priam to refuse: lucky for us.
One good attack, pushed then, would have destroyed
    us.

And afterwards our state was none too safe.
The pestilence that had begun at Aulis
Began again, and raged, and the Kings quarrelled.
Chances were missed and foolish chances taken
That ended ill: there was much bitterness.

It was a working life there, sieging Troy.
Sometimes we went on foray with the horse,
And gathered cattle, corn and wine and oil.
That was delightful to a lad at first.
But later, when the plunder had grown scarce,
And every raider had to fight for it,
Going, and gathering, and getting home,
It was rough service: needing many men.
Yet necessary service, for we starved else.

And when, after a night march and a raid,
And running fighting, driving back the cattle,
We entered camp, perhaps a gang from Troy
Would shoot into the camp and fire a ship.
Then out the parties had to go again,
To drive the bowmen back and quench the fire.
And when the darkness came we stood to arms
And slept upon our arms under our wall,
Those who were lucky: many watched, as sentries.

Then there was work: an everlasting work,
Mending the palisades, digging the ditches.
Digging the clearance channels after rain,
Unloading ships that brought us stores or horses,
Taking the horses to the tanks for water;
Going up river to cut forage for them,

And bearing back the forage under spear-shot.
Building and mending huts, bringing in wood,
Wood for the forges, wood for ship repair,
Barricades, palisades and burial pyres.
And daily fights and frequent night alarms;
And many night patrols and constant danger,
On scanty food and bad, in stench and flies;
Many men dying, very many sick,
None really well, and always in the need
Of showing we were longing for a battle.

Often they marched us to the city walls
"To show that we defied them," as they said.
It only made us envy them the more
Snug in their homes within the walls of Troy,
Singing (we heard them singing) and contemptuous.

Had they attacked us then, with all their strength . . .

And yet we hoped and longed to capture Troy,
To break them in a battle and so enter.
But with our quarrelling Kings what chance had we?

The prince Achilles quarrelled with Agamemnon
And would not fight, which meant, one third of us

Sulked in the tents, yes, even while the Trojans
Stormed over-thwart the wall to burn the ships.

For while Achilles sulked, the Trojan King
Put Hektor in command of all his host;
And then we suffered: night and day they raided,
Penning us into camp: and blazing arrows
Fell everywhere to set the ships afire.
And then all Troy burst on us and burst in;
They filled the ditch, they broke the wall, they entered
Right into camp; they killed men in the ships.
Had they but had another hundred men
And one half hour of summer daylight more,
They would have finished every man of us.
It was as near as that.   The darkness saved us.

Yet still Achilles sulked, with all his tribe.

He would have carried all his sulkers home,
Meant to, prepared to, but his friend was killed,
A fine young fellow, I forget his name.
I met him once.   He ventured out too far,
The Trojans got about him and so killed him
And took his armour.

                              Had they let him go,
I verily believe they would have won.

Achilles would have gone with all his men
And we without him should have had to go.
But no, they killed him: and Achilles' rage
Was like the fury of a god: he went
Straight against Troy, and slew and slew and slew,
Raging for vengeance, till he met with Hektor
And killed him underneath the walls of Troy.

And Hektor's death was blessed joy to us
And grief to them, but fortune changes face
Quickly in war: only a few days later
The Trojans killed Achilles in an ambush.
Our luck was gone that day and theirs was in.
We thought "Now Agamemnon will make peace."

And on that very night the Trojan Paris,
Who caused the war by bearing off Queen Helen,
Was killed patrolling at the Skaian Gate.
We said "Now this will certainly bring peace.
Helen will be returned to Menelaus."

The King sent into Troy suggesting peace
On that one point, that Helen be returned.
But young Deiphobus, Prince Paris' brother,
Said "No.   I swore to Paris to save Helen
From Menelaus always, come what may.

And so I will: she is my wife henceforth.
And Troy and I will keep her against all men."

He took command in Troy and stopped all thought
Of peace or treaty: so our Herald told us.

And Agamemnon knew that he was beaten.
For what with pestilence and mutiny,
His want of wit, and winter coming on,
There was no taking Troy.
                                    For, friends, remember,
Troy was a miracle of strength, with walls
Built by the gods themselves, as they maintained.

It was not so: they tricked Egyptian builders
To come to build them, and then cheated them.
But still, the walls were wonders of the world.

They were great, sloping walls of masonry
Twenty feet high, and on the top there stood
Twelve feet of upright rampart in addition.
Thirty-two feet of wall stood everywhere
All round the city, with square flanking towers
Jutting at intervals on every length.
Impossible to storm: we tried it once
And not one stormer of us reached the top.

Impossible to batter to a breach,
We had not men enough to do the work.
We and the ramparts being what they were,
We could not capture Troy, and knew we could
     not.

And so we growled, on this side mutiny,
While the Kings quarrelled, and the summer burned.

We did not know the truth till afterwards.
This is what happened.   Agamemnon called
A council of the Kings most secretly
Where they debated: "How to leave with honour,
Without disgrace, without a mutiny,
Troy being takeless and the winter coming."

Some were for crazy deed or crazy flight,
And Nestor wished that he were young again,
His usual wish, at more than usual length;
And nothing was decided in the end.
But when the Kings had gone, Odysseus said:
"Take this suggestion, mighty Agamemnon:
Send word to Troy that the Troy god Apollo
Has come to you in dream and ordered you
To end the war with Priam and begone:
That, before sailing, you and yours must make

An image of Apollo's sacred Horse
Precious with bronze and gold, in expiation
Of Greek pollution on Troy's holy soil.
That this great image should be left to Trojans
To drag into the city to the shrine
Of great Apollo.
                    That within few days,
Soon as this image has been wrought and decked,
You and your allies will break camp and sail.
That, in the meantime, all your Trojan prisoners
Will be released at once without a ransom.

For thus," he said, "you gain a holy warrant
For doing what you have to do, go home.
Epeios and myself will make the Horse.
Send you to Troy the message I have bidden,
Send it by all your prisoners released,
And tell the allies here that bright Apollo
Commands us to withdraw.   So trust Apollo."

Odysseus had his will: the King agreed.

So Agamemnon called his Trojan prisoners,
Told them what bright Apollo had commanded,
Promised the Horse, and sent them back to Troy
With gifts for each: and we were bidden launch

The ships into the sea, ready to sail.
And we were thankful to be going thence.

Then only, when Apollo's will was known
To Greeks and Trojans, was Odysseus' will
Made known to Agamemnon.

                    "King," he said,
"Inside the Horse we'll hide our champions.
The Horse will go into Apollo's temple:
The men will wait within him until cockcrow:
Then creep out of the Horse down to the gate,
Murder the keepers of it and unbar,
Our host, come secretly ashore again,
Shall be outside, ready to enter in.
The Trojans will be taken by surprise,
Utterly startled without will or way
They will surrender: we shall sack the city."

Men without plan succumb to any plan:
The King agreed to all Odysseus' plan.

Others will tell you of the Horse: myself
Only just saw him as I went aboard.
He was a stalwart stallion, plated over
With bronze and gold, upon a frame with wheels.

We left him in the ruins of our camp
And so set sail away from windy Troy.
What happened later, I will tell you later:
The story of the Horse waits to be told.

THE HORSE

My Father, King Epeios of the Islands,
Fashioned the Horse, after Odysseus' plan.
His shipwrights helped: this was the fashion of it:

The body of the horse was a hooped hollow
Of staves of wood, shaped to the horse's shape.
Within it, on each side, and at the chest
Were seats, covered with fleeces against noise,
To take five men, close-sitting two a side
Bent forward somewhat, and the fifth at end
Who sat more upright since his head had space
Within the horse's neck.

                    The entry hatch
Was in the beast's back, bolted from within
And covered with a saddle-piece of gold.

All this was made most secretly, unknown
By any, save Odysseus and my Father,
Who worked in a locked hut, under a guard,
"The work," they said, "being consecrate to god."

The pinewood workers made neck, head and legs.

Then all the parts were tenoned to each other
And treenailed fast, and shod to the wheeled stand.
Then the rough wood was polished with sea-sand
As smooth as ivory; then bronze workers
Plated the wood with bronze from battle gear
And ran fine goldwork over all the seams,
And horse-hair helmet-plumes made mane and tail.

When done, he seemed to march like a proud stallion
Bitted and decked, with an erect crest arched.

Then, when the Horse was finished, the five men
Were picked to go within: Odysseus, captain:
It was his plan; and he had been in Troy
A dozen times, dressed as a beggar, spying.
Next, Menelaus, as Queen Helen's husband,
The man with bitterest grievance against Troy.
Next, Neoptolemus, Achilles' son,
Longing to avenge his father, newly killed.
Next, Sthenelus, our best, after Achilles.
Lastly, my Father, who had made the Horse,
And claimed to share its fortunes.
                                        All these five
From gazing at the City, and from study
Of a model of the city walls and ways
Wrought by Odysseus out of river clay,

Learned all the alleys to the southern gate
That they would open . . . if their Fortune held.

My Father said: "I felt like to a swimmer
Who has betted all his having on the point
That he will swim a rapid, without harm,
And then, in the cold morning, sees the torrent
That he is pledged to swim, all jagged rocks
And gliddery boulders, antlers of dead trees,
Whirlpools and waterfalls and water-snakes,
Spikes, and a rushing shriek of bloated water,
Mangling and horrid death in every yard,
And dreadful hags of water with grey arms
Tossing to pluck him to their yellow teeth;
And wishes himself far, or the deed over. . . .

But still," he said, "Odysseus never doubted.
Odysseus said: "I answer for success
If once the Trojans bring us through the gates."

His captaincy turned doubt into a Hope,
And what the Hope became, another tells.

STHENELUS' DAUGHTER

The Entry into Troy

King Sthenelus, my Father, has often told me
The adventure of the Horse: I tell as he told.

"When the time came to put it to the proof,
Only we five and Agamemnon knew
What had been planned: then Diomed was told.

When the Greeks struck the camp and launched the ships,
We five went openly aboard a ship;
We said that we were bound to holy Chrysa,
To sacrifice to great Apollo there.
Men cheered us as we went and thought us gone.

But when we were beyond the Point, we landed,
And slept until a little before dawn,
When we returned unseen to Agamemnon,
And stole into the stable of the Horse.

There we anointed, prayed, and saw all ready
And took a meal together cheerfully,
Since it might be our last. Odysseus ordered

King Menelaus to the Horse's neck,
Himself to the King's right, me to the left,
Epeios on my left, facing the boy.
We waited for King Agamemnon's signal.

At the appointed time the trumpeters
Blew the long blast to bid the Greeks aboard.
There came a long long cheer and grating of pebbles,
And cheering and still more cheering.

                              We five shook hands
And said good-bye to light and clambered in.
When we were in our seats Odysseus drew
The cunning lid across and bolted it.
We were in darkness then, like five men buried.
Should we ever see the light of day again?

Then we heard Agamemnon at the hut,
Bidding men strike it: this was swiftly done.
Some glimmer of the daylight came to us.
Then workers felt about the Horse's body,
Fixing his golden trappings with small pins.
Then Agamemnon said: 'This Argive Horse
Is offered to Apollo's Trojan shrine.
We pray that Troy receive it and admit it
Within the shrine: and that it bring to Troy
The blessings that we pray for her: so be it.'

We heard him spill the wine in the libation;
Then the men muttered prayers: then the King
Ordered 'About turn. March. Aboard your ships.'
We heard the singing as they hoisted sail,
The cries of men heaving: the plash of oars:
The griding, rib on rib, the oaths and cheering:
And the crackle of the flames from the great bonfire
Of burning hut-wood well to leeward from us.
The noise of our friends' cheering slowly died,
We knew ourselves alone within the camp.

And then a crow perched on the Horse's head
And cawed and flapped, and cried an eager cry
Seeing a morsel, and with creaked wings went.

Then seagulls perched upon the Horse together:
They talked their sea speech as they preened themselves;
Then, after shifting leg for leg, they slept
There in the sun above us, while the heat
Grew greater in the oven where we were.

We five were packed into a narrow space
With fresh air only from the Horse's nostrils:
Outside the sun was beating on the wood
In full midsummer.   We had taken oath
Never to speak, but suffer silently

Whatever came: we panted: the sweat trickled.
Being so shut away, we could not tell
How long we had endured or had to suffer:
It seemed another life since the ships sailed.
Then suddenly Odysseus put his hand
Upon my knee: he had heard horses coming.

They were the Trojan chariots drawing near.

Our hearts thumped: the adventure had begun.

Then, as the horses and the chariots halted,
One of their stallions whinnied at our Horse.
We heard the men leap down to hold the teams
And the harness jingling, as the horses tossed.
Then Priam and the princes came about us.

And first they praised the beauty of the work.
'It was a well-made Horse, handsomely decked.'
But then one or two voices, which Odysseus,
Who knew Troy well, could recognise, not I,
Asked, 'Why should Agamemnon leave a Horse
Instead of gold or beasts for sacrifice?'
But Priam said: 'The god appeared to him;
Apollo's self ordered a Horse's image.'
One said: 'He bears at least ten pounds of gold.'

We heard the princes comment on our fleet
Now sailing past the Point to Tenedos.
And citizens of Troy came round the Horse
And stared and wondered at him; many praised.
They dared not touch, thinking him consecrated.
We heard them poking in the sites of huts
For relics of our stay, to carry home,
Spear-heads and arrow-heads and armour buckles.
Then Priam and the princes came again.
Then Priam put his hands upon the Horse
And shook, to test if it were strongly fixed.
He said: 'It is well made and heavy. Feel it.
The body must be made of solid wood.'
He tapped the body, but the plate and trappings
Made the blow dull. He could not prove it hollow.

We heard them bring up teams and waggon-traces,
Four teams were harnessed to the float, and men
Stood to side-traces and to guiding-traces.
Then, as the sweat came pouring down our faces,
We felt our prison moving towards Troy.

We were able to forget the heat a little
In the thought of what might meet us on the way.
My thought was, 'If the Horse break from its stand . . .
Or stick within the river at the ford . . .

Or fall and break asunder in the ford . . .'
But we had set ourselves upon the chance
And had to take what came.

It often happens
That a thing dreaded ere it come, is nothing
In the doing when it comes. We crossed the ford,
Scarce knowing we were there.

Long hours seemed to pass, then, suddenly,
There came a blast of trumpets and a cry,
A long wild cry of cheering and exaltation:
We were near Troy gate, and the citizens
Had crowded to the ramparts. We were there.

Here we were halted while they took the horses
And changed the traces for long ropes of leather,
Then all Troy's strongest, singing all together,
Hauled, and the girls flung flowers, pipers blew
Apollo's hymn, and so the Trojans drew
The Horse within the Waggon Gate of Troy.

Then our wheels rumbled on the paven ways
Up a steep slope: and ever hymns of praise
With lyres and with cymbals greeted us.
We went with music and with singing thus

Round all the city (to our seeming) thrice.
At the third round we thought: 'The sacrifice
Will follow this; shall we be burnt, or thrown
Over the walls to break upon the stone?'

We halted: then the singers ceased their song.
We felt that all about us was a throng
Of men and women pressing, touching, peering . . .
The heralds of the Trojans called a hearing.
When there was silence old King Priam spoke.
He was so near, we felt his left hand stroke
The Horse's neck and pat it when he paused."

My sister here shall tell you what he said.

THE TROJANS ABOUT THE HORSE

What Priam Said

"Apollo's self commanded Agamemnon
To make this image for the Trojan shrine,
In expiation of the long pollution
Of all Apollo's land by acts of war.
Here is the image, and the Greeks are gone
South of the headland, bound for Tenedos.
Now you, the elders, priestesses and priests,
Debate here in the council, and decide
What shall be done with this. There are three courses:
Bring it within Apollo's temple here,
Burn it with holy fire where it stands,
Or fling it from the ramparts to the rocks.
I urge that it be placed within the temple,
As bright Apollo bade the Argive King."

After a moment's pause another spoke:
"This city wants no offering from the Greeks.
This that the Greeks have made has been received.
I move that it be offered now to God
With holy fire, even where it stands.
When it is ashes, let us take the ashes

And fling them from the city to the wind,
And so be done with Greeks and offerings."

Another said: "We cannot understand
Why anyone should bring an Argive image
Into this city. We have suffered much
Since the first Argive image entered Troy.
We have her still, and suffer from the having.
I say let Princess Helen mount the horse
And ride on him over the walls to hell.
Then, when we have tilled the fields again,
Replanted all our vineyards, stocked our byres,
And put aside the memory of our sons
Dead in this war for Helen and her boy,
We may forget a little what we owe
To Agamemnon and his company.
At present we owe death to him and his,
And I say smash this image into fragments,
Here or upon the rocks below the walls."
And instantly the mob assailed the Horse
With tooth and hand, and would have torn it piecemeal
But for the press and the beast's size and strength.
But heavy blows fell on the beast, and hands
Snatched at the trappings, and a woman screamed
"Tear it to pieces, put it in the fire!"

We felt that we were ended, without hope.

Then, just as the Horse tottered under press,
There came something that made our blood run cold,
And checked the raging of those wolves of Troy
With horror.
          There came a cry like mad laughter or weeping,
A sobbing like one laughing over a corpse.
And the mob froze, and people shrank aside,
Horror had put her hand on everyone.
It was the worst thing that we suffered there.

KASSANDRA

I was the thing they heard, I am Kassandra.
I am as one blind from too much light.
The pure air, the pure light and the pure fire
And the ecstasy that comes, considering these,
Are all my having.   All else is touched with Death.

I saw that golden Horse, Apollo's Horse,
With all those Deaths about Him in Troy Town.
Men with their carrion arms and bloodstained hands,
And the skeleton fingers of the women stretched
And the skulls of all, all gibbering, showing teeth,
All rotting, all Death, about Apollo's Horse,
The stallion of Pure Fire on which He rides.
O terrible pollution, those living dead.

So I crept among them . . . and I am like the Light,
Death shrinks away from me, those shrank away . . .
I touched Apollo's Horse and instantly
Light came to me : I spoke the Light, the Truth.

This is Apollo's Horse.   Take off your hands
From this immortal work and holy gold.

This Wood is from the Holy Grove of Ida,
Where nothing mortal comes on foot or wing
Nor crawls, for it is lifeless, save for trees,
Pine trees immense, together ever-living,
A forest of the pine trees, nothing else,
Only the dark green trees, murmuring wisdom,
Daylong murmuring wisdom like the sea.

But at night, lo, they are mountain goddesses
Singing by moonlight terrible songs of god . . .
This Wood is of their Flesh, Goddesses' Flesh.

This Bronze, that was the armour of dead men,
Has since been through the fire, Apollo's fire,
The purity of fire has made it deathless.
This Gold is from the inmost mountain glen
Beyond all Life whatever, beyond all noise,
Save sometimes the rocks crack and the stones fall.

All day the rocks stand up among the glare,
All night they face the frost, the moon, the stars;
Not even the shadow of a cloud dare cross there.

And in its secrecy a water trickles
Out of the rock, the purest, brightest water,
Into a pool whose sand is dust of gold.
And there Apollo plunges from the rock.

34

This Gold is from Apollo's wing-feathers.

And Apollo will come into Troy at sunrise
To claim his Horse and ride: I see him riding
Bright, bright, bright, through the city . . .
                              O so bright . . .
Bright as pure gold: I see him riding here,
Brighter than gold, like something in a flame . . .
Yes, he will ride like fire, bright fire in Troy,
And, yes, the fire will redden as red as blood,
These ways, these walls, these towers, will glow like sunset,
A ruby of red, an ember, all heart's blood spilt.
And roaring fire will raven and lightnings sear.

His sword will bring bright death upon all of Troy;
O joy, joy, joy, when Apollo rides the ways.

> Bring precious gums, bring gold,
> The cobwebbed winejar old,
> The pure work of the bees,
> And Indian spice.
> Bring milk, barley, and oil,
> Bring salt, ashes and soil;
> Gather all these.
> We have a god to please,
> Apollo to appease,
> With sacrifice.

And strew down Indian silks, green silks, all woven
With sunbirds in gold thread, at the bright feet
That soon shall trample fire from the street
And dart his lightnings till the Wall be cloven.
Apollo shall come riding into Troy,
O joy, O joy.

Friends, beautiful Apollo tells me this:
That I shall ride on this immortal Horse
Far, far from Troy, in triumph, like a Queen,
Past lions, up a stair all strewn with purple
Straight into fire . . .
Straight to my lover Apollo waiting for me.

STHENELUS' DAUGHTER

In the Horse, till Sunset

That was the voice those hidden in the Horse heard.

She strayed back, lightly singing, to the temple.
My Father said, "Even within the Horse,
We felt the horror of those shrinking from her,
That priestess whom the god loved and had maddened.

After her song had ceased, King Priam said
'Draw this into the temple, as god bids.'

The men tautened the ropes to drag us in,
Starting a hymn, when a fierce voice behind us
Cried: 'I'll not welcome any Greekish gift;
Never. Let Agamemnon's Horse take that!'

And crash, a spear struck in the Horse's side,
Cracking the bronze and sticking in the wood.
Men wrenched it out and beat the flinger with it.

'Put him in bonds,' King Priam said: 'Sing on.
Bring bright Apollo's Horse into his home.'

37

We knew that we were dragged out of the light
Into a dimness sweet with burning gums.
We stopped: our dragging team unhooked the traces
And quietly went from us upon tiptoe:
We were within the temple: we were there.

Sweating and stifling as we were, we felt
Thanksgiving at our greatest danger over.
Fear having died, the hope of victory
Began to grow: our chance seemed to be coming.

The priests gathered about us with their incense.

Outside the temple there was still a crowd
Of men and women jabbering together.
Street-singers sang, and then the crowd would listen:
Street jokers, mountebanks and public mimics
Mimicked and mocked, and then the crowd would
    laugh
And then a man whose comrade had been killed,
And a half-mad woman, cried aloud again
For lovely dead lads lying in the rain,
And rage leaped up against the Greekish gift,
And grew, till the priests closed the brazen doors
And drew the bars: and then the rabble beat
Beat on the doors, crying, 'Have out that image.'

There was a passage from King Priam's palace
Into the temple. Priam's spearmen came
Into the temple by it as a guard.

And presently they cleared the crowd away
And kept the precincts free: we heard them pacing,
Shifting their spears, grounding their spear-butts,
    calling
'Stand back there, you. Keep back there. Stand
    away.'
Little boys shouted mockings and then fled,
And spearmen leaned their spears against the Horse:
They diced and joked and told each other stories.
One mounted on the Horse and switched and cried:—
'Get up now. Watch us gallop for the Cup.'
And we, half stifled in the Horse, were glad
Of anything that passed the time or showed
That time was passing. But the thought occurred
'What if these spearmen watch us all night long?
What if they sleep here, all about the Horse,
And take us as we open?'
                              But for that
We had small fear: the heat and the discomfort
And knowledge of the hours still to pass
Ere we could hope to stir, were pain enough,
We would face the other trouble when it came.

39   D

Then singing priests bore offerings in procession,
Men, women and children came with gifts.
Kassandra took them.   She offered them to god.

There was some little riot near the doors
During all this, but the guards silenced it.
Kassandra and the offerers withdrew;
The hours began again, of waiting, waiting.

The hours passed, leaving not even misery.
After long hours, it was sunset time:
We heard the water-sellers in the streets
Blowing their gurgling bird-calls and then crying
'Water; fresh Xanthus water; crystal water.
Fresh water from the Idan springs; so cold.
A penny the double-pitcher, but worth gold.'

It would have seemed worth minted gold to us.

One brought it to our sentries in the temple.

Then from the towers came the cry of 'Sunset.'
And trumpets blew the Closing of the Gates.
And every bell in Troy jangled or chimed
And children cheered: and women called to supper:
And men came thronging home: and shops were shut:

And the hammers that had beaten on the anvil
Since we reached Troy, were silent, we thanked god.
And almost instantly a coolness came,
And in the silence that fell suddenly
We heard again the never-ceasing wind
Running in every cranny, shaking shutters,
Flinging the dust against the masonry,
The wind of Troy, that blows all summer long."

In the Horse, Sunset till Cockcrow

"Then, to our joy, quick steps came up the courtyard,
A voice cried, 'Come, fall in, the First and Third.
Back to the Palace with you, into quarters.
The Second Watch will guard here until midnight.'

Then two out of the three watches of guards
Formed, and marched off: the third undid their cloaks
And slept upon the floor: all save two men,
A sentry, marching: and a sergeant pacing.
Sometimes the couple talked together there
(Leaning upon the Horse) of wine and women.

At the second changing of the sentinel
The priests entered with lights and sang their song

41   D*

How beautiful Apollo sailed the sea
In a red ship, into the midnight lands,
But soon would turn, and drive his flaming horses
Up from the world's rim, bringing light again.

Then, as they ceased their hymn, Kassandra came.
She stood beside the Horse next to Odysseus.
She said: 'The Trojan people are gone mad,
Quite mad, to bring this Horse into the City.
They should have burned it in the Argive camp,
Or burned it here, or flung it from the walls.
Apollo tells me truly; it brings Death,
A fivefold Death into the City's heart.
Death of the Man, Death of the Woman and Child,
Death of the Home they made, Death of the City.
Apollo says, *the image should be burnt
Even if it scream, like burnt men, in the burning;
As it will scream*, he says.

                                        Will you not burn it?'

'No,' the men said, 'the orders are precise . . .
To bring it here and guard it, until midnight.'

'But Apollo bids me say *it must be burned.*'

'Go, tell King Priam so, priestess,' they said.

42

'King Priam has forbidden me the palace
Because I am a priestess consecrate.
Go, tell him, you.'

                'We have strict orders, priestess,
Not to disturb King Priam before dawn.
When the King wakes he shall be told at once.'

She seemed to ponder this in agony.
Then she cried: 'Telling him at dawn will be
Too late for Troy: Apollo tells me truth.
I see nothing but burning: nothing but Death.

Then, suddenly, Kassandra struck the Horse
And cried: 'I name the fivefold Death within.
Odysseus, King of craft, hater of Troy;
Menelaus, who let Helen loose upon us;
Epeios, the contriver of the Image;
Neoptolemus, avenger of Achilles;
And Sthenelus, the Red-with-Trojan-blood.
These are the Deaths: Apollo cries *Destroy them.*'

She then went slowly back into the darkness,
Wailing *Destroy them. Burn the image now.*

When she had gone, the priests muttered their pity.
The spearmen murmured: then the captain said:—

'You priests ought to be guided by a warning,
Given by god; you ought to waken Priam
And tell him that the image must be burned.'

A priest replied: 'Kassandra has gone mad.
We cannot waken Priam for such madness.
He has forbidden us to listen to her,
Apollo speaks through the bright brain of man
Not through the clouded.'   ·
                                    Then the priests withdrew.

When they had gone, the captain said: 'And yet
I am for taking warnings sent by god.
I say we ought to send to tell the King.'

The guard agreed that Priam should be waked:
But who should wake that turbulent old King
Against his urgent orders: no man dared.
'But still,' the captain said, 'he should be told' . . .

While they debated, sentries on the towers
Blew a soft trumpet call and voices cried,
'It is now a rainless midnight and All's well.'

'Cease watch,' the captain said, 'To quarters. March.'

44

Those spearmen of the temple stood to arms,
Clashed their bronze spear-butts on the temple floor,
Shifted and turned and marched away from us:
And silence fell.
            We listened. All was still.
Then wise Odysseus swiftly drew the bolt
And thrust the hatchway up. 'Come on,' he said.
Those men will waken Priam and return
And burn the Horse: we have a moment's truce.'

He clambered out, we others after him,
So cramped, so stifled, we could hardly do it.
Odysseus snatched the weapons and the fleeces,
Reclosed the hatch, recovered it with trappings,
And whispered, 'Follow me: utter no sound.'

He led us deep into the temple's darkness.
There, at the north-east angle was a ladder;
He led us up it to a gallery,
Doubtless the passage to the treasure room.
'Drink, everyone,' he said, 'then lie and stretch.'

We drank the lukewarm water from our bottles
And stretched and felt new life come into us.

We had not lain five minutes at our ease
Before the guards returned, dragged out the Horse,

Smashed it with axes, in the temple close
And brought out blazing straw and burned it there.
Odysseus' wisdom saved us, barely saved us.

The fire from the Horse lighted the temple.
We saw the glare and people dodging by
Screening their eyes: within an hour it died,
Though smoke from smouldering embers blew about.
I was so weary that I slept: all slept
Except Odysseus: he kept watch for us.
And in my sleep I knew that Troy was quiet,
That danger was all past, or not yet come,
That of a hundred chances, ninety blessed us,
And that the long long trouble of the war
The toil, the watching, hunger, danger, death,
Loss of dear comrades, all these things, might end,
Soon end, in Victory, the lovely thing,
The spirit with the crown coming from Heaven,
Life after all that Death, Life, Life itself,
The Sun climbing aloft out of the Night.

And lo, in the dark rafters over us,
Within an unseen roost, Apollo's Herald,
A cock half-rousing, flapped his wings and crowed,
Crowed for the Sun still far under the rim
Of the dark land beyond Mount Ida there.
We waked at that clear summons of the cock.

'Come on,' Odysseus said. He led the way
Down, through the temple, through the open doors
Into the close, where still the embers smouldered,
And cats glided, and little Troy lay sleeping.

THE SURPRISE

You have heard the story of the Horse of Troy.

We left him on the sea-beach when we sailed.
We sailed all day, but when the darkness fell
The captains ordered all the fleet ashore.
We beached the black ships out of sight of Troy.

Then quietly the captains of the hundreds
Were told that a surprise would be attempted.
Orders were given: then most stringent watch
Was made, lest any traitor should give warning.

We supped and slept, till somewhere after midnight,
Then roused, and tied bleached linen on our arms,
And took short spears and swords: no other weapons:
And forth we went by fifties towards Troy.
Absolute silence upon pain of death
The order was: we crept along like ghosts.

Soon we were in the Plain among the graves
Of men half-buried, whom we used to know,
And how they died, a dozen known to me.
And Trojan bodies, too; familiar landmarks.

48

It was all cold and windy, with bright stars,
No moon, dry summer going, and the wind
Beating the withered grass and shrivelled leaves.
Then we were at the ford and passing through
I remember water gurgling at a flag-root.

Beyond the ford we were in Trojan land.
There was the black mass of the walls of Troy
With towers (and a light in one of them).
No other sign of life, except a glow,
Before Apollo's temple as we judged,
Some sacrificial fire not yet quenched.
The city was dead still, but for the wind.

They halted us below the waggon track
Between the Spartans and the Ithacans,
And there we huddled in the bitter cold,
Wondering what had happened in the city
And why the city should be still as death:
Whether the Horse were burning in the fire
With all our men inside it sacrificed:
Whether the trap door in the Horse had jammed
So that they could not leave it: or perhaps
(We thought) the Horse is guarded in the temple,
Surrounded by men praying all night long.
Or had they ventured out, and all been killed?

And if the men were killed, the stratagem
Was surely known, and we half-armed and freezing,
Would be attacked at dawn and ridden down.

A temple bell jangled within the city,
A lesser bell tinkled; then all was silent.

And all this time the little owls from Ida
Came hooting over us: and presently
A mighty, savage owl perched upon Troy
And snapped his iron lips, and flapped, and screamed,
Almost one saw the yellow of his eyes.
Then he launched forth, stealing into the air.

It seemed like many ages in the cold
Before the whisper reached the Ithacans
To creep a little nearer to the wall.
When they had passed, unchallenged, others went.
Word passed that there were sentries on the wall.

And though the orders were against all speech,
Yet whispers let us know that Diomed
Was at the South Gate underneath the tower,
With the picked fighters.
                              Hours seemed to pass
While we froze slowly in our companies.

My eyes were so accustomed to the dark
That I could see the great wall with its ramparts,
A tower, and a gate, close-fastened, brazen,
With men of ours heaped near it like to stones.

Then there was whispering in the ranks behind me:
A captain whispered, "Who knows Diomed?
Do you?" I whispered, "Yes."
                                    "Why, then," he whispered,
"Creep forward there, and find him by the gate
Under the tower with the forward party.
Tell him *King Agamemnon is convinced*
That this has failed, and that we must withdraw.
Be ready to fall back as we retire."

I crept the seventy yards up to the front,
One whispered, "Diomed is on the right,
Nearest the wall." I found him lying there
And whispered him the message of the King.
"What?" he said, "What? Withdraw from where we are?
Who says so? What authority have you?"
I told him, "Verbal orders from a captain."
"Lie still," he said, "And not another word.
I'll learn of your authority when day dawns."

Then suddenly there came a little noise.
Someone within the gate was lifting down

The heavy bars that barred it, one by one.
Each of us nudged his fellow and drew breath.
Diomed stood: we others raised ourselves.

One half the narrow brazen door moved back,
Showing a dark gash that grew wider and lighter;
A lamp wavered and flickered in a lane,
The damp glistened on wallwork; a man peered
Round the half-opened door ; and "Sst, Sst, Sst,"
He hissed. It was Odysseus, from the Horse.

Diomed signalled to us: he himself
Was first within the gate: I helped him there
To lay the gate wide open to our men.
Then we pressed in, up the steep narrow lane
Past the still flickering lamp, over a Trojan
Sentry or watchman, newly murdered there,
Killed by Odysseus: no one challenged us.
We were in Troy: the city was surprised.

The dogs had all been killed some weeks before,
There were no watch-dogs. When we reached the Ways,
The Wide Ways running round within the walls,
Some horses, tethered there, whinnied and stamped,
And drowsy horse-boys mumbled in their sleep,
But no one challenged; Troy was in a drowse

In the deep morning sleep before the dawn
Now faint upon the distant tops of Ida.

And we were seen by watchmen on the tower
On that side Troy, but none of them suspected
That we were Greeks: they thought that we were
   Lycians,
Old allies of the Trojans, mustering
Up to the temples for a sacrifice
Before we marched from Troia to our homes.

We were within the second ring of road,
Outside King Priam's palace and the temples,
Before a sentry challenged us, and then
It was too late for the alarm to help.
The man paused at the turning of his beat,
Looked round and saw us, gave a cry, then challenged,
Then died, stabbed through the throat by Diomed.

My party rushed into Apollo's temple
And burst into the palace to the guards
Sleeping in quarters, some of them half drunk,
All without arms: we herded them like sheep.

And by the time the guards were bound, the city
Was lit with blazing thatches, and awake,

Dawn coming, fire burning, women screaming,
And war-cries, and loud trumpets and clashed armour.
There was hard fighting in a dozen spots.

We came out of the guard-room by a gate
Into a blaze all red with fire flying:
A palace court it was, the inner court,
Where Menelaus and his Spartan spearmen
Were killing Priam's sons.
Just as we reached the court a dozen spearmen
Were all attacking young Deiphobus.

I knew the lad by sight, for he had come
On embassy to Agamemnon once,
And Menelaus meant to have him killed
And flung to the camp-dogs, because of Helen.

There he was, fighting for his life with twelve.

A fine young man, like Hektor in the face,
A bright, clean-cut face, tanned with sun and wind,
Smiling and cool and swift with parry on parry.

He had been surprised: he had no body-armour,
Nothing but spear and shield, and there he stood,
Checking each thrust, swift, marvellously.

One minute

He stood, matchless in skill in the red glare,
Then someone crept above and stabbed him down.

The city was all ours in the hour.
Many were killed in fighting: many more
Escaped, during the burning and confusion,
Out, to the mountains, by the Eastern gate.
The rest we took: some of the prisoners,
The little children and old men and women,
We drove out of the gates into the wild.
The rest we kept; young women skilled in crafts
And men who might make slaves.
                              We made them quench
The fires that were burning here and there
And then we sacked the city utterly.

When we had sacked her utterly, we forced
Our Trojan slaves to lever down the ramparts
Over the walls, until the city seemed
A mound of fallen stones and roofless houses.
We lit the wreck.

Then as we sailed for home with slaves and plunder,
We saw the ruins burning, and the smoke
Streaming across the sunburnt Trojan plain.
With all that world of murder on our backs
We bore our load of misery from Asia.

EPILOGUE

Spoken by Kassandra

Though many died and many fled
To live as beasts do, without bread,
Or home, or bed,

Yet many, like myself, am slave,
Weeping the life the spirit gave
Into the grave.

However long our lives may be,
There is no hope of getting free
To such as we.

Swallows will come again, and flowers,
Not Troy, who guarded with her towers
That life of ours.

What help in giving way to tears?
To those most hurt by Fortune's spears
A spirit nears.

EPILOGUE

The spirit whom the prisoner knows,
And broken wretches faint from blows;
It comes most close.

And though I tread the unknown stair
Up, into Death, I shall not care,
It will be there.